Goldwin Smith

A Letter to a Whig Member of the Southern Independence Association

Goldwin Smith

A Letter to a Whig Member of the Southern Independence Association

ISBN/EAN: 9783744765091

Printed in Europe, USA, Canada, Australia, Japan

Cover: Foto ©ninafisch / pixelio.de

More available books at **www.hansebooks.com**

LETTER

TO A WHIG MEMBER OF THE SOUTHERN INDEPENDENCE ASSOCIATION.

A

LETTER

TO

A WHIG MEMBER OF THE SOUTHERN INDEPENDENCE ASSOCIATION.

By GOLDWIN SMITH.

BOSTON:
TICKNOR AND FIELDS.
1864.

AUTHOR'S EDITION, FROM ADVANCE SHEETS.

UNIVERSITY PRESS:
WELCH, BIGELOW, AND COMPANY,
CAMBRIDGE.

A Letter to a Whig Member of the Southern Independence Association.

MY DEAR ———

You and I have some political principles in common, and there is therefore no absurdity in my attempting to reason with you on a political question as to which we happen to differ. Your Association wishes this country to lend assistance to the Slave-owners of the Southern States, in their attempt to effect a disruption of the American Commonwealth, and to establish an independent Power, having, as they declare, Slavery for its corner-stone. I am one of those who are convinced that in doing so she would commit a great folly and a still greater crime, the consequences of which would in the end fall on her own head. If you were an enemy to free institutions, and a lover of " Slavery, Subordination, and Government," I should at once understand your position, and despair of moving you from it by any arguments of mine. But as you are a friend to free institutions, at least up to the measure of 1688, I do not so entirely despair of offering you such reasons as may at least induce you to hesitate before you plunge your country into an American war. For it is towards war that you are now driving. You are doing your utmost to facilitate the escape of the Confederate iron-clads from the Mersey. One of the most eminent of your number has given notice of a motion in Parliament, evidently having this end in view. And if these vessels are allowed to go out, you do not doubt, I presume, that there will be war. Indeed, you must be conscious that bare recognition, the ostensible object of your Association, would be futile, or rather would enrage the Federals, and determine them to persevere. Suppose Ireland were in rebellion, what effect would the recognition of the insurgent government by a foreign power, say France, produce on the temper of the English nation? Would it make us more willing to yield the victory to the insurgents, and to acquiesce in the disruption of our empire?

The course taken by the Government has unfortunately been such as to give the attempts of your Southern friends and their allies to embroil us with the Federals a very fair chance of success. They have declined to take their stand on the firm ground of international duty, which plainly forbids us, as professed neutrals, to allow either belligerent to make our shores the base of his maritime operations, and have taken their stand instead on the ground of municipal law, which is wholly irrelevant as between nations, while, at the same time, they have shrunk from amending the municipal law in the manner required in order to render it equal to the present need. The consequence is, apparently, that only the law's delay (a most humiliating protection) is now interposed between us and a calamity which even those who are doing their best to bring it on us, would almost fear to name.

You perhaps think that because the Americans have already a war upon their hands, they will tamely see their ships burned and their commerce destroyed by vessels cruising from the ports of an ally. If the Commonwealth has men of spirit, and men who know their duty, at her head, rather than see her suffer such dishonor, they will see her in an honorable grave. But, judging from experience, I think you much miscalculate the habits of nations when they are once roused to a certain pitch of frenzy by a desperate struggle for existence. The French Republic, when we attacked her, had two great military powers already on her hands. She was besides bankrupt and torn by civil war. Yet she was ready to fly at the throat of another enemy. And the victory over the revolutionary levies of a nation driven to despair, which seemed so sure and easy, cost us, as we know, twenty years of war.

Let me first tell you why it is that I feel the interest which I do not wish to disguise in the fortunes of the Commonwealth which you are so anxious to break up. It is not from a fanatical love of what are commonly called Republican institutions, or from a desire precipitately to "Americanize" any country which is not yet ripe for the largest measure of self-government. A man must have read history to very little purpose if he has not learned that political institutions must vary according to the character, intelligence, and social condition of a nation; and that all are equally beneficent after their kind, which at a given time, and under given circumstances, suit the requirements of the people. Would that our statesmen, who turn Indian Zemindars into squires, and press upon the untrained Greeks a parody of the English Constitution, were a little more conscious of this great truth. The Americans, for their part, seem not wholly unconscious of it. Though Republicans themselves, they show no fanatical hatred of our monarchy. They receive the heir to the English throne with demonstrations of enthusiastic affection, and I believe Queen Victoria reigns in their hearts as completely as she does in ours.

Indeed, if my heart were set upon a republic of the classical kind, — the republic of Brutus and Cassius and the debating-clubs, — I should look for it in the seceding States, or anywhere rather than in a land of political equality and social justice. The classical republics were based on Slav-

ery: the political character of their citizens **was that of**
a dominant caste maintained in proud idleness by the labor
of servile hands: and this character is avowedly imitated by
the Southerns, though more successfully in point of courage
and military vigor than in point of cultivation and refinement.
I wonder it has never occurred to those who were exulting
over the **failure of** republican institutions, and in the same
breath lauding the **political** greatness of the South, that the
South also is a republic, with exactly the same constitution
as the North in all essential respects, saving the article which
prohibits the Southern Congress from passing any law deny-
ing or impairing the right of property in negro slaves.

My reason for feeling a deep interest in the American
Commonwealth is this: It seems to me that the aim of all
social effort, and the object of all social aspiration, is to produce a real community, every member of which shall fully
share the fruits **and** benefits of the social union.   I say this
in no communistic or revolutionary sense, but in the sense
in which it must be felt to be true by all, whether Liberals
or Conservatives, who are trying to improve the condition
of the poor, and especially by those who are doing so in
obedience to the social principles laid down in the Gospel.
Such is the goal to which the progress of society, through
all its various and successive phases, would seem to be tending, if it is tending to any goal at all, and is not a mere blind
and aimless current.   That English society in its present
state is very far from having reached this goal, is what you
will scarcely think it Jacobinical to assert.   It is an open
question among writers on economical history whether the
mass of the peasantry in this country have really shared at
all in the increase of wealth and comfort which has accrued
to the upper classes in the course of the last three hundred
years.   No one will venture to say that they have shared in
anything like a fair proportion.   Too many of them are still

in a state of great misery, of brutal ignorance, and of the vice which misery and ignorance always bring in their train. Millions of our laboring population live constantly in view of penal pauperism, and nearly a million of them on the average are actually paupers. They pass through life without hope : they die in destitution : the only haven of their old age, after a life of toil, is the workhouse. In most cottages of many counties the children are under fed that the father may have enough to work upon : and any physician who has been much among the poor will tell you that numbers of them die in their infancy from want of proper food and clothing. In Ireland, centuries of horrors to which, I say most deliberately, history affords no parallel, seem to be closing in the expatriation of a people. There is wealth, luxury, and splendor, such as perhaps the world never saw, in the palaces of our nobles and our wealthy merchants and stockbrokers : but there is hunger, and the horrible diseases that wait on hunger, at the palace gates. Pass from the dwellings of the rich to those of the poor, and you will own, that though we may be a great and powerful nation, a community in the full sense of the term we are not. These things are freely stated and even exaggerated by Conservative writers whose object it is to disparage the present in honor of the past ; and I do not see why it should be treason to state them when the object is to prevent the same party from destroying the opening prospects of the future.

While the mass of the people have so little interest in the existing state of things, and while they are at the same time so wanting in the education and intelligence requisite for the exercise of political rights, our statesmen naturally shrink from giving them the franchise : though all of us, even the strongest Conservatives, are conscious that it is not a just or sound system under which the bulk of the community, while they bear all political burdens, while they pay heavy taxes

1 *

and shed their blood for the country in war, are excluded
from all political rights. A fraction of our citizens (if it is
not a mockery to use the term) enjoy the franchise. The
rest enjoy what even the leader of the Conservative party
has derided as the ironical franchise of "virtual represen-
tation"; that is to say, they are left in the hands of classes
whose interests are often quite different from theirs. Great
progress has been made since the Middle Ages in every
respect, except perhaps the more romantic qualities, among
the upper classes of society: but the condition of the unen-
franchised laborer, if you look at the real facts, instead of
being satisfied with the mere name of freeman, is little
above that of the mediæval villain. He is even still, under
the Law of Settlement, in some measure bound to the soil.

No man who loves his kind, and feels that his own happiness depends on the happiness of his fellows, can desire that
such a state of things should be final. No man of sense and
reflection, **I believe,** imagines that it will be so.

Now, in the American Commonwealth, partly I grant by
the bounty of nature and the lavish fertility of a virgin
world, but partly also, I think, by institutions, especially by
those regulating the distribution of land, and by the thorough
diffusion of popular education, one portion at least of these
evils, the poverty of the masses, has been to a great extent
removed. The laborer in America, in a material point of
view at least, is prosperous and happy. He is the possessor
of property : he has no fear of dying in the workhouse, or
of seeing starvation and destitution round his death-bed. If
he is industrious and frugal, he has all the world before him ;
and however ambitious he may be, however high he may
look, hope **still cheers** him on, for he sees one of his **own**
class in the foremost office of the state. This you will say
is a coarse happiness, falling far short of high civilization.
Still it is something, as the world moves slowly, and it is the

basis of all the rest : for though man does not live by bread alone, he must have bread to live. Property confers dignity and self-respect : the hope of rising in the world sustains frugality and self-denial : the removal of physical misery stanches the greatest source of crime. Of the fact that the laborer is more prosperous in the Free States than in this country, and that one step in the improvement of man's lot has at least been gained, the vast emigration from this country to America, which continues unabated in the midst of civil war, is in itself a conclusive proof. The number of emigrants will go far towards making up to the North for the loss of life in the war, at least according to a rational estimate of that loss, though not according to the estimate of public instructors, who, to produce a budget of gratifying horrors, set down all the soldiers whose term has expired as killed.

As to the political part of the grand experiment : before we estimate its result, we must in fairness make allowance for some heavy drawbacks. We must make allowance for the violent bias towards the democratic side given to the States, at the outset of their career as a nation, by their struggle for freedom against the monarchy and aristocracy of this country. We must make allowance, as I believe, for some mistakes committed by the founders of the Constitution under the influence of European prejudices, especially the institution of an elective President, as the republican counterpart of a king ; which, though it has accidentally been of great service in this extremity, by giving the nation a sort of constitutional dictator, is, under ordinary circumstances, a dangerous stimulant to senseless faction and personal ambition. We must make allowance for the turbid tide of wretchedness and ignorance which is poured into the American community by the government of this country, and with which, I think, candor must allow that American institutions have dealt wonderfully well. We must make allowance for the want of that experience from which we received many a severe and chastening lesson before our political character was moulded, and which the Americans are now undergoing, for the first time, in a stern form. Above all, we must make allowance for the presence of Slavery, shooting moral and political poison through every vein of the State ; and for the influence of the fell alliance between the Slave-owning Aristocracy of the South and the Democratic party in the North, — a tyranny, deliverance from which would be well purchased even at the price of a civil war. No doubt there have been great evils and gross absurdities in American politics. There has been factiousness, though, perhaps, scarcely greater than that of our own political parties, under their historic and aristocratic leaders, in the matter of Parliamentary Reform ; there has been corruption, though, I fear, not worse than there was in our own legislature, when the holders of political power, peers as well as commoners, were selling their support to railroads ; there has been a flux of Parliamentary rhetoric, less refined, certainly, and possibly less instructive, than the debates of our own House of Commons; there has been demagogism of a very repulsive kind, though, if it were not an ungracious task, it would be easy to show, by examples on this side of the water, that aristocracies have their demagogues as well as mobs. As to journalism, the New York Herald is always kept before our eyes; but the New York Herald is not the American press : and I most firmly believe that neither this nor any other American journal ever pandered to the violence of the rowdies more vilely, either in point of virulence or mendacity, than a great English journal has pandered to the hatred of America among the upper classes of this country during the present war. Some of us at least have been taught by what we have lately seen not to shrink from an extension of the suf-

frage, if the only bad consequence of that measure of justice would be a change in government from the passions
of a privileged class to the passions of the people.

After all, the American Commonwealth has, in part at
least, solved a great problem for humanity. The full rights
of citizenship have been conferred on a whole people ; a
real community has been called into being : and yet order
and property are, as the rapid increase of wealth proves,
at least tolerably secure. American institutions have received that which is the best practical stamp of excellence,
— the loyal attachment of a perfectly free people ; and we
have learned what, considering the doubtful aspect of political affairs in Europe, all who are unbiassed by class prejudices will be glad to learn, that society may repose on liberty
as a sure foundation, and that the people, when moderately
educated, will obey authority which they have themselves
bestowed, and reverence laws which they have themselves
enacted. The American Government calls upon its citizens
for the tribute of their blood; and that tribute is not with-
held. The charge of carrying on the war with Irish and
German mercenaries is cast upon the Federals by an aristocracy whose armies have been filled both with Irish decoyed
into an alien service, and with mercenary Germans bought
like cattle for the shambles. But the commissariat and the
military hospitals of the North are of themselves enough to
show that the war is not being waged with vile and mercenary lives. If you wish to know the signs of a war waged
with vile and mercenary lives, read, with attention to the
hospital and commissariat details, the military history of
the European powers, — of Austria, of Russia, even of England, till something of a democratic spirit arose and enforced
regard for the soldier as well as for the general. Recollect
the treatment of our sailors which brought on the mutiny of
the Nore. The American soldiers are highly paid, no doubt ;

but wages in their country are very high, and they are fighting without medals or ribbons, and without the lash.   There
has been a good deal of drafting ; but there are also a great
many volunteers : and, on the whole, the armies are, to a
great extent, citizen armies, such as no Government not
deeply rooted in the affections of the people could have at
its command.

Military power is commonly thought a great test — by
some the greatest test — of the excellence of political institutions.   If this be so, American institutions must be entitled
to some respect.   For I believe no nation in history has
ever, by its own resources, kept armies so large, so well ap-
pointed, and so well supplied, for so long a time in the field.
Nor has there been any signal break down, like that of Bal-
aclava, in the military administration, though the scale of
operations has been so colossal, and the field of war so vast.
It is true that private zeal has come to the aid of the Government, especially in the hospital department ; but this is a
part, and a very striking part, of the political system ; and
you will observe that in this case it is loyal co-operation, not
ambitious and disloyal rivalry like the Crimean Fund of the
Times.   Military skill and discipline are not created in a day
among a people devoted to peaceful industry, and brought
up in a freedom and equality which unfit them for the command and the obedience of the camp.   But these qualities
seem to have arisen with reasonable speed.   I doubt whether
Europe could show a nobler soldier in any point of military
character or duty than General Grant, who declines to come
forward for the Presidency against Mr. Lincoln, because, if
he did so, he would be placed for six months in a position
of rivalry towards his superior in command.   With Meade,
Rosecranz, Banks, Thomas, Sherman, Grierson, Gilmore,
Dahlgren, Farragut, and others who could be named, little
fault is to be found : and how many great commanders did

England produce under the aristocratic system, during the
first five years of the Revolutionary war? The practical
result is that half of the task which European soldiers and
statesmen pronounced impossible has been accomplished,
and the remainder brought at least within the limits of pos-
sibility. So far I think you must go with me. I do not expect you to go with me in saying that the nation as a whole
— particular cases of misconduct, failure, or folly being set
aside — has shown during this struggle, at least during the
latter part of it, and since adversity has laid her chastening
and elevating hand upon the people, the true, though rugged
lineaments of greatness. It has risen after terrible defeat
elastic and indomitable. In its darkest hour, though its language, like ours, was querulous and desponding, it has not
lost confidence in itself. It has not lost even a kind of grim
good humor, the sign of a strong heart. It has wisely stood
by its Government, though its Government was not always
wise; and has not passed votes of want of confidence against
Ministers just struggling out of their early difficulties in the
middle of a war. It has quelled party spirit, strong as the
party spirit there is, in face of the common enemy, with a com-
pleteness which fills its enemies here with impotent and ridiculous rage. It has gone forward, or is now going forward, and
bearing its Government forward with it, as one man, with a
unity which I believe has scarcely ever been equalled in history, except perhaps in the case of the French Republic,
where it was produced by Terror. We have always been
told that the men of intellect and refinement in America stood
aloof from politics in sullen disaffection : but during this struggle they have equalled or surpassed the rest of the community
in devotion to the common cause, and to the " rail-splitter "
who is its constitutional chief. The President himself was
chosen out of the mass by the ordinary method of election,
not called forth to meet a terrible emergency ; yet he has

met the most terrible of all emergencies with sense and self-possession, as well probably on the whole as it would have been met by any European sovereign or statesman whom you could name. Military merit, whether of the President's party, or, as in the cases of Grant and McClellan, of the party opposed to his, has been promptly recognized and heartily supported. No commander has been removed till he had really failed, in which case commonwealths consider the safety of the soldier as well as the feelings of the general: and (which is a very significant and noble trait) those who have been removed, after failure, from supreme command, have for the most part continued to serve the government of their country loyally, cheerfully, and well, in a subordinate position. Personal ambition and personal rivalry have in the main been held in check by the public good; and the cause and the commonwealth have been supreme. At the outset there was a frightful amount both of corruption and of treason: but, as it seems to me, both have a good deal abated as the struggle has gone on, and as the face of the people has grown sterner. All wars breed contractors; and if you wish to see that commercial selfishness and covetousness are not confined to America, you have only to look at the great English shipbuilders, who are ready to plunge their country into a dishonorable war rather than lose a customer and forego the addition of a few thousands to their already enormous wealth. Great emergencies bring out without disguise all that is noble and all that is base in man: and the baseness is apt to appear first.

The worst part of the case, and that of which the aspect is in all respects most sinister, undoubtedly is the finance; as to which it can only be said that the burden laid upon posterity is not so heavy, especially when regard is had to the boundless resources of the country, as that which has been laid by other Governments for objects in which posterity had infi-

nitely less concern ; and that the nation will probably be helped
through this, as it has been helped through other difficulties,
by the strong sense of a common interest which pervades all
its members, and by the cordiality with which, at need, it
supports a Government which is not separate from it and
above it, but an embodiment of itself.

If you do not go with me in thinking that the Americans
have shown military greatness, still less, I fear, will you go
with me in thinking that their attachment to freedom has
stood the strain of civil war. You are probably convinced
that liberty has given way either to an anarchy or to a
tyranny, though you scarcely know to which. The correspondent of the *Times*, as that journal assures us, has been
living under a reign of terror unparalleled in history ; unparalleled certainly, since under no previous reign of terror has
a man been able to publish, with perfect freedom and in perfect safety, the most violent and calumnious denunciations of
the terrorist Government. The tacit consent of the nation
has placed in the hands of the President extraordinary
powers for the suppression of the treason with which, at first,
the North swarmed, while the enemy was at the gates of the
capital. Those powers have, in some cases, been arbitrarily
used. But, generally speaking, personal liberty has been
secure to a degree unequalled, I venture to assert, in so fearful an extremity ; to a greater degree than it **was here**
under Pitt, in an extremity far less fearful: to as great a
degree, to say the least, as it is now under the Italian Government, which, under the pressure of similar necessity, has
assumed similar powers, and is in like manner charged with
the most tyrannical atrocities by the enemies of the Italian
cause, and the friends of the Bourbon despotism and its
dungeons. The tyrant Lincoln, though " worse than Robes-
pierre," will very likely be re-elected President by the free
suffrages (you will scarcely deny that they are free) of the

oppressed people, or of so many of them as have survived his
guillotine. The exercise of political rights in all the States
not under military occupation has been unrestrained ; the best
proof of which is, that at one time the elections went very
much against the Government. As to the Constitution, it
has never been in danger for a moment, except in the eyes
of the Southern party here, whose wishes fathered the strange
thought that McClellan of all men in the world was going to
play the part of Bonaparte ; and the disappointment of all
such expectations, when they had been so confidently ex-
pressed, and seemed so well warranted by the analogy of
European history, must be taken as a proof that, in the judgment of its enemies, the love of liberty among the Americans
is strong, and capable of resisting forces which have ship-
wrecked the liberties of other nations. The truth is, that
beneath the troubled and unhealthy surface of general politics
there has always been at work the quiet and healthy influence
of the local institutions, which have really formed the political character of the people. There has been no tendency up
to this time to lapse into sabre sway; the soldiers have
retained apparently all the sentiments of citizens; and the
President Commander-in-Chief has grasped at the first opportunity of restoring civil government in Louisiana and the
other States won from the Confederates ; a proceeding for
which he is, of course, denounced by those who had just
before been railing at him for attempting, as they said, to
overthrow civil government, and to rule by the sword. But
he has probably learnt by this time that it is vain for him to
aspire to the approval of the editor of the *Times*, and that he
must look for the sanction of his measures to his conscience
and his country. And the name of the editor of the *Times*
reminds me that the anarchical despotism of the American
press, of which we have heard so much, has proved not to be
above reasonable control. We have seen nothing like the

Times's expedition to Sebastopol, or the editor's letter to Sir
Charles Napier, ordering him to attack a fortress which was
pronounced impregnable by the most daring of living seamen.
The generals have also been allowed, feverishly anxious as
the people were for news, to put a tolerable check on the
revelations of newspaper correspondents.   This ungovern-
able nation has shown at need strong instincts of government
and sufficient powers of self-control. I see no reason for dis-
claiming kinship with these people. So far as I can discern,
they are true Anglo-Saxons in a burning vessel, between sea
and fire, fiercely agitated, of course, but still masters of themselves.

Perhaps nothing has practically done the Americans more
harm, in the opinion of this country, than the want of taste
shown in their documents and speeches. When men are
fiercely excited, their language is apt to correspond to their
emotions; and the postures of a nation wrestling for life are
not likely to be regulated by the rules of grace. Besides
this, however, taste is the prerogative of high education, such
as falls to the lot, even in this country, of the wealthier
class alone : and the education of the Americans is notori-
ously rather general than high.   Their energies hitherto
have been employed in reclaiming a vast wilderness, and
laying the solid foundations on which we have no reason to
doubt that a graceful superstructure will hereafter be reared.
We have no reason to doubt this, I say, since already there
exists — not indeed in the Slave States, which in this respect
seem hopelessly barbarous, but in the Free States — a liter-
ature of high value in all departments, as well as eminently
pure. In practical inventions the Americans are supreme :
and they are most ready to borrow from us the fruits of pure
intellect, which they will one day perhaps return with interest. Our great writers, who look so coldly on them now,
and whose coldness they feel so keenly, have only to go

among them to discover that want of respect for intellectual eminence is not among their faults. The beginnings of all civilization are deficient in refinement: those of the feudal civilization, in which we still linger, were coarse enough; and surely it would be fastidiousness with a vengeance to reject or attack the real cause of humanity on the mere ground of want of taste in its defenders. As to boastfulness, it is highly offensive and generally indicative of weakness. The Americans doubtless needed such a lesson as they have received to cure them of it, as well as of other tendencies which are incident to unalloyed prosperity. But are we ourselves free from it? Is it not exactly the fault of which all the world accuses us? What are the Russian guns planted before the towns of this country but boastfulness; and boastfulness, to tell the truth, of a rather ignoble kind? By what else than appeals to that which, in the case of the Americans, we should call boastfulness, has the present leader of our nation risen to so high a pre-eminence above all the statesmen of his time?

The experiment which is being made in America for the benefit, as it seems of mankind in general, (at least of those who have no particular class interests and look only to the general good,) is twofold. The Americans are trying not only whether society can be placed on a broader, and, as most men would allow, sounder and juster, basis than that of opulence ruling over pauperism; but whether religion, when deprived of the support of state authority (a support which you must see is beginning to prove not adamantine), can rest securely on free conviction. Whether this part of the experiment has succeeded or failed, is a question far too large to be dealt with here. It is clear that religion, though free, retains its hold upon the nation. The voluntary payments for the maintenance of churches exceed in amount the revenues of the richest establishment in the world. There is a good deal of religious zeal, combined, if De Tocqueville may be trusted, with full social toleration. Theological questions excite great interest; and the theology of the Americans, if less learned than ours, and inferior in literary qualities, is more robust, grapples more vigorously with great questions, and is therefore more likely in the end to lead to truth. Appeals are made in extremity to the religion of the American people — and even, in spite of the diversity of sects, to its common religion — as confidently and with as much success as to ours. The conflict between religious principles and material objects in a great commercial nation is severe; but though we are far removed from the days of the Puritan fathers and their " plantation religious," it cannot be said that religious principles **have as yet** succumbed.

The best index, after all, of the influence of religion, is the national character: and the severest tests of national character **are** pestilence and civil war. All civil war is horrible. But I confidently assert that this civil war has so far been, on the part of the North, without exception, the most humane in history. We scarcely need a better proof of the fact than the perpetual harping on the proclamation of Butler, which, after all, was only words, and would have been soon forgotten in presence of very bloody deeds. In our own civil war, which was far more humane than those of Rome, Greece, France, or any other country however civilized, Essex, the finest gentleman as well as one of the most gallant soldiers of his time, when asked by the Queen **for a** safe-conduct, she being ill after childbirth, answered her with an unfeeling jest. **I** need not remind you of the atrocities which attended the **storming of** Drogheda and Wexford on the one side, and that of Leicester on the other. Excesses have been committed by the Federal armies. Excesses are committed by all armies in an enemy's country. Excesses of the most horrible kind were committed even by

our own armies on these very scenes. Confederate property
has been destroyed by Federals on land, while Federal property was being destroyed, and in a way peculiarly barbarous
and exasperating, by the Confederates at sea. These
ravages, and expressions of ferocious hatred, for which, I
think, I could find you parallels not excused by the frenzy
of battle on this side of the water, seem to be the chief of-
fences of the North. We have heard of no denial of quarter, no maltreatment of Confederate prisoners, and assistance
has been given without distinction to the wounded of both
sides. No language, so far as I am aware, has ever been
used so disgraceful as the yell for "revolutionary energy,"
that is, for indiscriminate burning and massacre, which arose
at the time of the Sepoy revolt from the infuriated and panic-
stricken population of Calcutta. The Chairman of your
Manchester meeting tells us that this is the most ferocious
war that has been waged for a century. Not to mention the
Spanish civil war, in which the aged mother of a chief was
put to death and horribly avenged, or the days of June at
Paris, when no quarter was given, and poisoned lint was
sent to the wounded, — the Irish Rebellion of 1798 falls
well within a century. Read the account of the reign of terror, — the scourgings, half-hangings, pitch-cappings, picket-
ings, rapes, burnings, plunderings, massacres, carried on by
the Anglo-Irish aristocracy and their satellites during the
viceroyalty of Lord Camden. Read it not in Rebel histories,
but in the correspondence of brave and loyal soldiers, such
as Cornwallis and Abercrombie, who turned away sickened
from the sight, — and learn how terrible and how difficult
to control are the passions of civil war. Butler has gone un-
censured : so did Anglo-Irish terrorists ten thousand times
more infamous. The wrongs of the Irish people were
brought under the notice of the House of Lords ; but the
House of Lords, bishops and all, turned a deaf ear to the

complaint. The riots and massacres at New York were ingenuously charged on Northern ferocity. They were got up in the interest of the South by Southern agents, and they were perpetrated by Irish rowdies, fresh, as most of the rowdyism is, from the misgovernmnnt of other countries. I may be mistaken, but I cannot help thinking that even a certain affection for the Southerns has continued to exist in the hearts of the Northerns through all the fury of the fray : respect for the military heroism of the South certainly has not failed. The chief organ of your party proclaimed with great exultation, that the hearts of the Northern women were in favor of the South, and against their own husbands and brothers. This was a fiction invented to gratify the generous tastes of the circle in which these writers move; but it is true that both sexes in the North have regarded Southern valor as half their own; and this feeling will be a healing influence when the hour of reconciliation arrives. That any blood will be shed upon the scaffold when the war is over, that any policy will be pursued but that of general amnesty with very limited exceptions (exceptions in the case of men whose ambition has sent hundreds of thousands to their graves), no one for a moment imagines. And the absence of such apprehension is a strong proof that the spirit of humanity has not lost its power.

This estimate of the American institutions, and of their effect on national character, as shown under the trial of civil war, is of course open to dispute : it rests partly on evidences which are at present incomplete, and will not be complete till the end of the war. I do not expect a man of Southern leanings to accept it as true. I only ask him to consider before he plunges us into war with the Federals, whether in that storm-tost vessel, which with straining planks and in imminent danger of wreck, holds her course against wind and sea, there may not be embarked, as I firmly believe there is,

something in which humanity has an interest, and which no
man but a very narrow-minded member of a privileged
order or church would willingly see perish. I only ask him
to consider whether in the course of Providence it may not
have been given to the peasant founders of New England,
as well as to the followers of Hengist or Clovis, to open a
new order of things, not without benefit to large classes to
whom the old order of things had not been so kind; and
whether, if this be the case, an attempt on the part of those
who profit by the old order of things violently to crush the
new order, lest by its success it should ultimately imperil
the continuance of the old, would not be rather selfish, and
even rather unsafe.

The Americans, I fully grant, were entitled to no sympathy while they remained accomplices in Slavery. You
might admire their marvellous energy, industry, and national
prosperity. You might see with pleasure the improvement
of the laborer's condition in the Free States. You might
own that the desire of territorial greatness, to which they
sacrificed their moral greatness, was natural and almost
universal. You might hope, and even feel sure, that the
day would come when they would find by bitter experience that Freedom and Slavery could not dwell together,
and when, rather than sink under that deadly tyranny, they
would risk the loss of territorial greatness. You might
mark that conscience was not dead among them, but lived
and struggled in a party which resigned the hope of political
power that it might be true to Abolition. But you could
not regard them as representatives of the rights of labor, or
of political freedom, or of any other great principle, before
the world. Now, however, the day long foreseen has arrived. The Slave-owner, no longer able to tyrannize under
the forms of the Constitution, has appealed to force, and
Freedom and Slavery are grappling in mortal struggle for

the possession of the New World. In the sufferings of the
war the Free States expiate the apostasy of the past. Take
care you do not lead us into the same apostasy, and into as
bitter an expiation.

As to this war, no one was more opposed to it at the outset than I was. I too, though in the interest of the Free
States, would have said, *Part in peace;* not seeing, as the
people with their sounder instincts have seen, that between
nations formed by a violent disruption, and divided by no
natural boundary, there would be no peace, but perpetual
hatred, constant wars, and standing armies, the scourge of
industry and the ruin of freedom. I thought the task of
subjugation hopeless, suicidal, and therefore criminal. I
knew from history the tremendous strength of slave Powers,
in which the masters are an army supplied by the slaves
with food. I knew also the vast extent of the country to
be subjugated, and the difficulties which it presented to an
invader. I knew that the power of the slave-owning oligarchy of the South would enforce a unity in their councils
and actions, which the parties of the free North would be
long in attaining; and that though there was a loyal party
in the South, as the very process of Secession and the voting
at the Presidential election proved, the strong arm of the
oligarch would put down all dissent. I did not know, for in
truth we had never fairly seen, the power of a great and
united nation, every member of which was a full citizen, and
felt the common cause to be entirely his own. Yet there
was a precedent in history which might in some measure
have furnished a key to the probable result. We are all
taking on this occasion nearly the same side which we
should have taken in our own civil war in the time of
Charles I., excepting perhaps a part of the shopkeepers,
who in those days had strong convictions, but who in these
days have no very strong convictions, and are led to take

2

the side of the South because they fancy it to be genteel.
That civil war was marked in its course by nearly the same
vicissitudes as this.   The Commons, superior in numbers, in
wealth, and the material of war, fell with overweening confidence on the Cavaliers.   But the Cavaliers had at first the
advantage in military spirit and in the habit of command,
while the retainers whom they brought into the field were
better trained to obey.   Edgehill was not unlike Bull's Run.
One wing of the Parliamentary army galloped off the field
without striking a blow ; and Clarendon declares that, though
the battle began on an autumn afternoon, runaways, and not
only common soldiers, but officers of rank, were in St. Alban's
before dark.   Then followed despondency as deep as the
previous self-confidence had been high and boastful.   Overtures were made to the King, and Pym and Hampden, the
" rabid fanatics " of that day, had great difficulty in prevent-
ing a surrender.   Nor was treason wanting, in camp or
council, to complete the parallel.   Still darker days followed; and when the King sat down before Gloucester, the
friends of " Slavery, Subordination, and Government," at
that time, must have felt as sure of victory as they did when
General Lee was approaching the heights of Gettysburg.
But our Puritan Fathers had the root of greatness in them ;
and therefore they were chastened, not crushed, by adversity. Necessity brought the right men to the front, and gave
the ascendency in council to those who were fighting for a
principle, and who knew their own minds.   The armies,
which at first were filled with tapsters and serving-men,
were recruited from the yeomen, of whom, with their small
estates, there were plenty in Old England; but who, since
the soil of Old England has become the property of a few
wealthy men, have found another home in the New.   The
moderate commanders who did not mean to win, gave way
to commanders who did.   Treason was trodden out and

disunion quelled.   There was no more boastfulness, no
more despondency, but stern resolution.   The **Commons**
measured their work, settled down to **it**, and won.   **We**
deem **that** struggle heroic, and feel a mournful pride in looking back on it: but **you** cannot be familiar with **its** history,
if you do not know that it had its wicked, its mean, even its
ridiculous, as well as its heroic, phase ; or think it impossible
that, when removed by the lapse of centuries from close
inspection, the struggle which **we** are now watching may
appear quite as grand.

It was reasonable too, I think, **to feel** great misgivings —
I know that I at least felt them — **as to** the object of the war
and **its issue, supposing the North to** be victorious.   **I ex-
pected,** and the language of **the N**orth warranted us **in**
expecting, reconstruction with **Slavery,** and the restoration
of that baneful tyranny, inexpressibly worse than any number of disruptions.   Indeed, I am quite ready to admit that
it was only in the course of the war, and as the fact that
Slavery was the incorrigible source of disunion, as well as
of all other political and social evil, was brought home to
them, that the majority of the Northerns resolved on its
destruction, and that Emancipation became the policy of the
nation.   But that Emancipation is now the policy of the
nation, — even of old Democrats such as General Grant, —
there can be no doubt whatever.   Every additional year
of war places reconstruction on any basis but that of immediate or speedy Abolition, more completely out of the question.   Nothing but the victory of the Slave-owners can save
Slavery from destruction.

I will add to these reasons for having been originally
opposed **to the war,** the very deep horror with which all I
ever heard or **read** has filled me of wars in general, and the
strong sense which I have of the fact, that, under the modern
system of standing armies, those who to gratify their own

passions plunge nations into wars, and who swagger about
national courage and national honor, do not risk their own
lives, but sit safe at home, and bravely send poor peasants,
ignorant of the quarrel and utterly unconcerned in it, to
bloody graves, — a fact which I beg you to bear in mind
with reference to warlike members of our own Legislature,
and clergymen who wish to embroil us with the North, as
well as with reference to the warlike orators and preachers
of the United States. But the war has been begun, and is
now probably drawing towards its close, whatever its des-
tined issue may be. We are not responsible for it. The
only question is whether we shall interfere, and (if Slavery
is wrong) on the wrong side.

The grounds upon which the Southern Association appeals to this country are succinctly set forth in the Address to
the Public, which is evidently the work of a careful as well
as a skilful hand. Let us pass them very briefly in review;
always remembering that the present object is practical, and
that it is not to dissuade you from sympathizing with the
insurgent aristocracy of the Southern States, which would
neither be a very hopeful nor a very fruitful undertaking,
but to inquire whether you have any rational pretence for
calling upon England to deviate from the principle of not
interfering, for class or party purposes, in the internal revo-
lutions of other countries, to which we have pretty steadily
of late years adhered, after trying the opposite course, and
finding that it cost us dear.

"SOUTHERN INDEPENDENCE ASSOCIATION OF LONDON.

"Public opinion is becoming enlightened upon the disruption of the
late United States, and upon the character of the war which has been
raging on the American continent for nearly three years. British subjects were at first hardly able to realize a federation of States each in

itself possessed of sovereign attributes; while deriving their views of American history from New York and New England, they ascribed the secession of the Southern States to pique at a lost election, and to fear for the continuance of an institution peculiarly distasteful to Englishmen. Assurances were rife from those quarters that the movement was the conspiracy of a few daring men, and that a strong Union sentiment existed in the seceding States, which would soon assert its existence under stress of the war.

" Gradually the true causes of the disruption have made themselves more and more manifest. The long-widening and now insuperable divergence of character and interests between the two sections of the former Union has been made palpable by the facts of the gigantic struggle. Their wisdom in council, their endurance in the field, and the universal self-sacrifice which has characterized their public and their private life, have won general sympathy for the Confederates as a people worthy of, and who have earned, their independence.

" On the other hand, the favorable judgment which Englishmen had long cherished as a duty towards that portion of the United States which they imagined most to resemble the Mother Country has met with many rude shocks from the spectacles which have been revealed in that land of governmental tyranny, corruption in high places, ruthlessness in war, untruthfulness of speech, and causeless animosity towards Great Britain. At the same time the Southerners, who had been very harshly judged in this country, have manifested the highest national characteristics, to the surprise and admiration of all.

" Public men are awakening to the truth that it is both useless and mischievous to ignore the gradual settlement of Central North America into groups of States, or consolidated nationalities, each an independent Power. They feel that the present attempt of the North is in manifest opposition to this law of natural progress, and they see that the South can never be reunited with the North except as a conquered and garrisoned dependency; whilst the Northern States, if content to leave their former partners alone, are still in possession of all the elements of great and growing national power and wealth.

" Our commercial classes are also beginning to perceive that our best interests will be promoted by creating a direct trade with a people so enterprising as the Confederates, inhabiting a land so wide and so abundant in the richest gifts of Providence, and anxious to place themselves in immediate connection with the manufacturers and consumers of Europe.

" In short, the struggle is now felt to be, according to Earl Russell's pregnant expression, one for independence on the part of the South, and for empire on the part of the North; for an independence, on the one hand, which it is equitable for themselves and desirable for the world they should achieve; for an empire, on the other hand, which is only possible at the price of the first principles of Federal Republicanism, and whose establishment by fire and sword, and at a countless cost of human life on both sides, would be the ruin of the Southern States. These, surely, are reasons which invoke the intervention of other Powers, if intervention be possible, in the cause of common humanity.

" Therefore, not in enmity to the North, but sympathizing with the Confederates, the Southern Independence Association of London has been formed, to act in concert with that which is so actively and usefully at work in Manchester. It will serve as the rallying-point in London of all who believe that the dignity and interest of Great Britain will best be consulted by speedily and cheerfully recognizing a brave people sprung from ourselves, speaking our language, heretofore organized for internal government into well-established sovereignties, now confederated under a stable Central Administration, and claiming recognition, in accordance with those principles of British policy which have always been more inclined to help the oppressed than to justify and abet the oppressor, and ever to respect a unanimous national will.

" The precedents of the separation of Belgium and of Greece, and of the reconstruction of Italy, exist as modern instances to show that Great Britain is always ready to acknowledge, rather than to resist, a national uprising. It would be difficult to show that any of these countries was as well organized for self-government as the Confederate States have now been for nearly three years. Unlike them, each State of the Confederacy had its own constitution and government complete and in working order, and had ever since gone on acting upon them without change or difficulty.

" The Association will also devote itself to the cultivation of friendly feelings between the people of Great Britain and of the Confederate States; and it will, in particular, steadily but kindly represent to the Southern States that recognition by Europe must necessarily lead to a revision of the system of servile **labor unhappily** bequeathed to them by England, in accordance with the **spirit of the age, so as to combine** the gradual extinction of slavery **with the** preservation **of property, the** maintenance **of** the civil polity, **and the** true civilization **of the Negro** race."

The Committee, **the** names **of** whose members are appended, is highly aristocratic in its character. The List of **the** Members of the Association, which has also been published, contains a large proportion of men of title and family, whose names head the list, and a good sprinkling of clergymen, curiously associated with the Member for Sheffield; but it is not so strong in representatives of **the** interests of the laboring class.

We need not dwell long on the opening paragraphs **of the** Address. **The** question **now before** us is, **not** whether the struggle ought to have been commenced, but whether this country ought to interfere in it. But even writers who most intensely hate the Federals, and most violently condemn them for persevering with English tenacity, and in spite of all disasters, in the gigantic task which they had undertaken, allow **that** originally the right was on their side, that **Lincoln's** election was perfectly constitutional, and that he had done no single act to provoke rebellion against a Government which the present Vice-President of the Confederacy had himself pronounced to be, in its general character, the most just and beneficent in the world. Your own Address in effect confirms this judgment; for it ascribes the rebellion to a diverg-**ence of** character and interests which has gradually come to **light in the course of** the struggle, and which therefore can hardly have been its original justification, much less a ground **for condemning the** President's **attempt** to maintain, as was his bounden duty, **the** integrity of the nation constitutionally committed to his hands. As to the power of secession at will, and without provocation, British subjects might well find a difficulty, as you say they did, in realizing a community founded on so singular a basis, more especially as the United States had dealt with us, as well as with all other countries, and entered into perpetual and indefeasible treaties with us as a single Sovereign Power.* The Constitution contained no article of the kind, and you will scarcely require us to believe, though I have seen it suggested, that the framers were so fatuous as to omit the mention of this fundamental right, and make no legal provision for its exercise, leaving the nation to the chances of violent disruption and civil war, for fear of suggesting the topic to men's minds ; as though (not to mention the other absurdities of such a course) anything could be more suggestive than so conspicuous an omission. But even if a legal right of secession existed, this was not an exercise of it. This was a conspiracy hatched with all the incidents which mark the proceedings of conspirators, and under circumstances of peculiar perfidy arising from the position of the authors as the elective rulers and guardians of the state. One of the leaders writes to his confederate to suggest secret dealings with the national armories for the purposes of the plot, and ends his letter by describing himself as a " candidate for the first halter." Is this the language of men preparing to exercise a legal right?

Some of your party seem to think that a president has not a right, like a king, to put down unprovoked rebellion. They appear to regard a commonwealth as the offspring of political crime, in which no legal authority can reside. You, as a Whig, will not agree with them ; more especially as you must see that no form of government but a commonwealth being possible under the conditions of American society, to

---

* If I understand the theory rightly, Maryland and Virginia might have seceded at will, and cut off the capital. A central State, commanding indispensable lines of communication, would thus be mistress of the existence of the nation.

deny that lawful authority can reside in such a Government would **be to** proclaim perpetual anarchy in America. **Nor** will you maintain that a Government which had its origin in a just rebellion is thereby disqualified from putting down a rebellion which is unjust. You know too well that our Government had its origin in the just rebellion of 1688. The noblemen and clergymen of this country, in their passionate hatred of a free community, the success of which they suppose to be fraught with eventual danger to social and ecclesiastical privilege, are tearing up the foundations on which not only all privilege, but all society rests. They are inciting to treason and insurrection all sections of any community which may think that there is a divergence of interest and character between them and the rest of the nation. Such a facility of political divorce might not be without danger to the union of the "Two Nations" which the Tory author of Sibyl has described as existing with totally divergent characters and interests in this country. It would have warranted the Free Traders of the North of England in declaring themselves independent of the Protectionist South: indeed, according to the theory which was elaborately propounded as a subterfuge for English morality in sympathizing with the Slave-owners, but which seems now to have served its turn, the difference between the Free Traders and the Protectionists was the great cause and justification of this secession. As to the principles on which the integrity of the British Empire reposes, our aristocracy has given them to the winds. It has left itself without the shadow of a warrant for coercing Ireland, in case of a general rising in that country: and, Heaven knows, in that case the divergence of character and interests, (if that is a justification of rebellion,) is wide enough.

However, I will freely admit that the rebellion was caused by a divergence of character and interests, not between the

2*　　　　　　　　C

mass of the people North and South of a certain geo-
graphical line (for Western Virginia did not secede, and
other Southern districts seceded only under pressure), but
between the Slave-owners and the mass of the people. This
collision had long been foreseen by all observers, and it has
come at last. So long as the Slave-owners could command
a majority in Congress, and elect a President of their own
by the help of the party connected with them commercially,
or under their influence in other ways, they were content to
remain in the Union, though they were alarmed, and justly
alarmed, by the growth of moral sentiment, and the increas-
ing efforts of the Abolition party in the North. But when
the Republican party triumphed in the election of a President, they felt that the hour for which they had long been
secretly preparing was come : they rose in arms and dragged
with them into insurrection the free laboring population en-
closed within the limits of their power. The danger which
had long been threatening Slavery from the spread of the
Abolition doctrines and the attitude of the Abolition party in
the North, is the sole cause of secession alleged in the
secession Ordinances, and the sole motive for secession dis-
closed in the Confederate Constitution, which follows the
Federal Constitution in all essential respects, except that it
includes special clauses protecting, as a fundamental article of
the Confederation, the property of the master in the negro
slave, and removing the limits which the Federal law set to
the extension of Slavery into new States. The insurrection
followed exactly the winding boundary line of Slavery, passing between the slave-breeding part of Virginia and the free-
labor part of the same State ; its focus was in the centre of
Slavery, and its intensity was graduated in different parts of
the insurgent territory, according to the prevalence of the
Slave or Free interest. Its outbreak was attended by new
developments of the Slavery doctrine, of the most startling

kind, and by apocalyptic visions of a vast Slave empire
stretching from the tomb of Washington to the palaces of
Montezuma, while it was not attended by any new developments of economical doctrine, or by any visions of emanci-
pated trade.   In fact, I must do the ambitious leaders of the
revolt the justice to say, that the idea of destroying the ma-
jestic fabric of the Union for the sake of a tariff is more
congenial to the mercantile genius from which the theory
emanated than to the aspiring spirit of President Davis or
General Lee.

I agree with the Slave-owners in believing that the Abo-
litionists of the North were sincere, and that Slavery was in
real, though probably not in immediate, peril : and, if we
set aside the immorality of their institution, I am not sure
that self-preservation might not fairly be pleaded as in part
an excuse for what they have done.   It might have been
pleaded, perhaps, with more justice if the extension of
slavery, as well as the maintenance of it where it exists,
had not been part of their design.   They cast the die, however, well knowing that they staked all upon the event;
and they have not been sparing of the lives or fortunes of
others in playing out their game.   The result has been to
bring destruction, in all probability, on what with a delicacy
of expression almost Southern you call " an institution peculiarly distasteful to the English people."   I hope, indeed, that
the institution in question is still peculiarly distasteful to the
English people, in spite of the efforts which have been made
in a great variety of ways to reconcile them to it; and
therefore I hope, and am confident, that the people will decline your invitation to interfere, at the risk of war, for the
purpose of saving it from its approaching fall.

No doubt the Federals, in proceeding, against all expec-
tation, and, as I have before confessed, to my dismay, to
coerce the Slave-owners, were actuated by very mixed mo-

tives. There was a desire to prevent, on moral grounds, the establishment of a Slave Power, and to save the negroes from being swept away into hopeless bondage, of the sincerity of which the fear of Abolition which drove the Slave-owners to **revolt is, as** I said before, a sufficient proof. There was the desire which all loyal citizens feel to punish treason and put down unprovoked rebellion. There was **the** desire (not, perhaps, altogether wise, but neither altogether unnatural, nor altogether criminal) to preserve the greatness of the Union. There **was** anger, not philosophic, but such as treachery, violence, and insolence will awaken in mortal breasts; there was mortified vanity; there was pique at the shout of exultation raised by the enemies of freedom in Europe over the ruin, as they thought, of the great Commonwealth. The less worthy motives predominated, perhaps, at the beginning of the contest; the worthier, I think, have been gradually gaining the ascendency as it **has** gone on. But in deciding whether we shall interfere on the side of the South, we must look to the practical interests of humanity, which I suppose you admit to be on the side of Free Labor, not to the motives of the North. Are **we** to make England an accomplice in the creation of a great Slave Power, and in its future extension from the tomb of Washington to the palaces of Montezuma, because the motives of those who are fighting against it are not altogether unalloyed?

I have admitted that there is a divergence of character as **well as of** interest between the Slave-owner and the free laborer, or the employer of free labor. The Slave-owner always has **been**, and always will be, a despot, incapable of living on equal terms with other men. But there is no divergence of character such as would be a bar to political union between the whites of the South who are not Slave-owners and their kinsmen (for nobody but a man laboring under rhetorical frenzy would deny that they are kinsmen) at the North. The whites of the South have been taught to spurn labor as degraded, and have themselves been degraded by so doing. But this war, if I mistake not, by placing them under military discipline, has raised their character, and made them more capable of living under law; while the destruction of Slavery will necessarily convert them into free laborers of some kind, or employers of free labor.

Suppose the Emancipation policy to be carried into effect; suppose the Slave-owning aristocracy, which will not live with freedom, which " hates everything free, from free-schools upwards," to be abolished, and its members reduced to the level of citizens, I see, judging from the experience of **his**tory, no impediment to the complete and permanent restoration of the Union. Though civil war is so fierce, its wounds are soon healed. People who must live together, and trade and intermarry with each other, cannot long keep up mutual hatred. Sadness will take the place of harsher feelings; and in the present case, as there have been victories on both sides, and each side has had cause to respect the valor of the other, the quarrel will not be kept alive in the heart of the vanquished by the rankling sense of humiliation. The first patriotic object, the first struggle with a foreign enemy, which reawakens national feelings, will probably complete the cure; and neighboring powers must beware of the tendency which has so often been shown, to bury the memory of civil in foreign war. The few years of Cromwell's Protectorate, though following a most bitter and protracted civil war, and themselves full of partial insurrections, plots, and decimations of the vanquished party, sufficed to bring about reconciliation to a considerable degree among the great body of the people. Not many years since, a part of the Swiss Confederation seceded from the rest in the cause of Jesuitism, which had disturbed the peace of that community, as Slavery has disturbed the peace of the Union. The other cantons marched upon them, coerced them, expelled the Jesuits, and restored the Confederation. Complete reconciliation ensued, and of that quarrel, I believe, there is now no trace.

No doubt the Union party in the South has for the time been effectually crushed by the strong arm of the oligarchs; but it does not follow that Union sentiment is extinct, or that it will not revive if the power of the oligarchy is overthrown. In the Southern as well as the Northern States, there prevails, Slavery apart, a strong desire for a wide and united empire as a source of strength and greatness. This desire is so strong, that very good judges, thoroughly acquainted with the Southern States, thought it would bind the North and South together, in spite of the manifest tendency of Slavery to rend them asunder. You hold it to be for the interest of "your own dear country" that a disruption should be effected, and that the great power of the American Commonwealth, which we choose to think and do our best to make hostile to this country, should be broken in two. So said the Noble Chairman of your Manchester meeting, discarding for a moment the language of disinterested sympathy with the patriotism and heroism of the Slave-owners, and allowing a less romantic but more natural motive to appear. I hold this motive for taking the wrong side in the greatest moral struggle, and the most pregnant with future good or evil to humanity, of our days, to be as baseless as it is selfish. I maintain that, class interests and class fears being set aside, there is no reason why the English people here should regard with apprehension the greatness of the English people on the other side of the Atlantic; or why their greatness should not be to all intents and purposes a part of our own. But be this as it may, it is clear that the final disruption which the enemies of American greatness, for their purposes, desire to promote, the friends of American greatness will in

the same degree desire to avoid : and that the Southerns as .
well as the Northerns are friends to American greatness.
If you wished to render the restoration of the Union impossible, you should have **been more cautious** in disclosing the
diplomatic object of your sympathy with the South.

It is as needless as it would be odious to discuss the truth
of the comparison which you draw between the character of
the Federals and that of the Confederates. For you cannot
seriously expect the Government to take a dangerous step
merely on the ground of your personal predilections. It
must strike you as singular, that the line of demarcation
which separates perfect virtue from perfect vice should exactly coincide with Slavery. **You** judge the conduct and
language of the Federals by **an** unfair standard ; by the
standard of nations living in peace and tranquillity, **not** by
the standard of nations whose fiercest passions are stirred to
their depths by a terrible conflict, and who are surrounded by
the atmosphere which, charged with fear, suspicion, false ru-
mors, and wild hopes, hangs over revolutionary war. Name
any other great civil war in history, and, if its details remain
to us, I will undertake to show you that your special con-
demnation of the Americans is unjust. You have, moreover, been prevented by the intensity of your prejudices
from noting the change which has been wrought in the character of the people under its trials, and you take as true now
all that might have been true at the date of Bull's Run,
when the Americans were but just entering the fiery fur-
nace through which they have since passed. And further,
your accounts of the untruthfulness of speech and the other
crimes with which you charge a whole nation of the same
blood as our own, are taken, I have no doubt, from a **journal**
which has itself, through the whole of these transactions,
been a palmary instance of untruthfulness of speech, and
of everything else which can degrade the calling of a pub-

lic instructor. "Few journalists," says an English periodical of Southern leanings, "have ever incurred greater responsibility than the New York correspondent of the Times. It is on his testimony alone that a large and most influential class of English society has sympathized with the South. He has throughout acted the part of an unscrupulous advocate, carefully reporting to his employers, and through them to all England, every statement and every fact which could create contempt and disgust against the conduct, the principles, and, in general, the cause of the North. He has uniformly represented the Federalists as tyrants, marauders, curs who bought Irishmen and Germans to fight their battles, fraudulent bankrupts, and odious hypocrites. Of course he is not abusive: 'Our own correspondent' never is; but in a quiet way he reports every discreditable fact, every dirty job, every harsh or cruel act in the conduct of the war; he quotes every blackguard rant of the New York Herald, and he leaves out of sight all that is heroic or pathetic." *   The writer proceeds to show, that, considering the difference between American manners and ours, the undoubted existence of a great "blackguard element" in New York, the disorder necessarily incident to an immense army raised in a few months, and the unexampled temptation held out to jobbing by the enormous and sudden expenditure, "nothing could be easier than to misrepresent the whole aspect of the war, without saying a single word that was not either true or at all events attested by plausible evidence." Not that the Times has confined itself to misrepresentation of this kind.   Its readers still, I presume, believe, on its authority, that the Admiralty cases in the United States are sent to be tried before a low attorney; and that Mr. Wendell Philips has withdrawn his son from the conscription, though Mr. Philips has no son, a fact of which the editor of

* Fraser's Magazine, October, 1863.

the Times was made aware. Even Mr. Reuter's telegrams were too impartial, and others were substituted, in which mere vituperation could be given as authentic news. We have strong reason to think that the correspondents wrote to order, unless their reports were tampered with; for one of them has published a work on his own account giving a picture of these transactions very unlike that which was given in the Times.

While the Slave-owners were loyal to the Union, nothing was too bad to be asserted and believed of them. The Times could even swallow the delirious figments of a lunatic who fancied that he had seen horrible murders and ferocious duels committed with perfect impunity in the carriages on their railways. It is only since they have become the destroyers of the Union that they have appeared to our enchanted eyes paragons of every public and every private virtue. The Southern Correspondent of the Times is a person whose history is well known to the public, and on whose representations reliance cannot be safely placed. The character of the "mean whites" in the South seems, as I said before, to have been improved by military discipline; and the whole Confederacy, under the rule of a strong oligarchy, has shown extraordinary vigor in war. The valor of the troops has been sometimes sullied by great ferocity, especially in their treatment of negroes in the Federal service. This is really all that we know at present. To talk of "private virtue," as the special attribute of the Slave-owners and their dependents, is surely to leave the evidence far behind.

You speak of the causeless animosity of the Federals towards Great Britain. To have your merchantmen burnt, and your commerce driven from the seas, by vessels issuing from the ports of an ally, sailing under his flag, and manned with seamen belonging to his naval reserve, — to have his

Parliament loudly applauding the builder of these vessels, and exulting in the ravages which they have committed, and this in spite of your having honorably done your duty in like cases to him, — to see an outlying fort of his on your coast covering with its guns a swarm of blockade runners to feed the resistance of your enemy and protract to you the expenses and sufferings of war, — to be assailed day after day, not only with the most rancorous and insulting abuse, but with the grossest calumnies, by newspapers which are universally and justly regarded as the organs of the English upper classes and of the English Government, — to be called the scum and refuse of Europe by a member of the English Legislature on a public occasion, and in presence of a Prime Minister whose own language and actions in Parliament indicate that he sympathizes with the sentiment: — all this may not be thought an adequate cause of animosity, but that it is a natural cause you will hardly deny, unless you deem all commonwealths too vulgar to be allowed to feel an insult. The Americans, as new-comers, have been too sensitive to the opinion of historic nations, especially (in their hearts) to the opinion of this country, and too anxious for foreign applause. They want a history of their own, and henceforth they will have one, to banish this childish vanity and put manly pride in its place. Meantime their language, even the language of their public men, has sometimes been such as to degrade the grandeur of their efforts and sully the goodness of their cause. But they had a fair right to be surprised and indignant, when they found, or thought they found, that we sympathized with the Slave-owners, — we who gave ourselves out to the world, and were always applauding ourselves as the great crusaders against Slavery, and who were arrogating extraordinary powers and doing high-handed and obnoxious things all over the ocean, as the professed champions of the antislavery cause. Their feelings toward us have been greatly improved, and their language has become more courteous since they discovered that the malignity which finds its organ in the Times was that of a party and not of the English people.

You may persuade yourselves that your hearts were on the side of the Free States at first, and that the conduct of the two parties in the struggle has compelled you reluctantly to transfer your attachment to the Slave-owners. But you will not so easily make us forget the books and pamphlets teeming with hatred of the Republic which were published by some of your number at the very beginning of the war. And so, when you protest that you are not actuated by enmity to the North, you ought to tell us what other emotion than enmity, such language as "scum and refuse of Europe," "more degraded than the Mexicans," is intended to express. If we are to deal out charges of hypocritical lying against a whole nation, we must at all events take care that all is perfectly ingenuous on our side. The excuse, however, which you tender for your sympathy with the Slave-owners at least implies an admission that there is something in it needing an excuse: and if the members of the aristocracy who head your Committee some years ago cherished the love of freedom as a duty, they will be able to make allowance for those who have not yet learnt to regard it as vulgar fanaticism and canting hypocrisy, or ceased to look upon a Slave Code which denies to a whole race not only lawful marriage, the right of giving evidence in a court of justice, and all the other rights of man, but the education which might raise the slave above the level of an animal, and the hope of emancipation, as one of the most terrible monuments of deliberate wickedness which the world has ever seen.

Pursuing the course of the argument in your Address, we come next to the proposition, that Central America must, by the laws of nature and for the good of its inhabitants, (and also, as has been candidly said, " of our own dear country,") be split up like Europe into a number of independent nations; a truth to which you say public men are awakening, and which they find it impossible any longer to ignore; though I trust they may find it possible to leave nature to carry into effect her own laws on the American Continent, as she will assuredly do in the long run, without the officious and superfluous aid of British arms. This idea, however, that the European system must be reproduced in America, though very natural, is, I suspect, in Baconian language, an idol of the cavern, — a fallacy of the narrow European enclosure by which all our ideas are bounded, as those of the Siamese king were bounded by his Siam. The political progress of humanity through a series of successive phases, down to our time, is manifest enough. Why are we to suppose that it will not continue? And if it is to continue, what absurdity to act as though the order of things in which we happen to live were final, and to be forcing it, as the last achievement of exhausted Providence, on a new world. Multiplied centres of thought and action, at once stimulating and moderating each other, sustaining emulation, and furnishing comparative experience, are probably as desirable in America as in Europe : but it does not follow that they are to be produced exactly in the same way or at the same expense. In Europe they are produced by a division of the Continent into independent nations, based, generally speaking, on differences of race and language, and involving a corresponding division of interests and a liability to international disputes, which can be settled only by the arbitrament of war; whence the curse of standing armies, with which political liberty has scarcely found it possible to exist. But in North America, inhabited by people of one language and, if not originally, by fusion, of one race, the same end may be attained, without the same liabilities, by the system of federation, which seems designed by nature to bind the rising communities of the New World together in a Union combining all the political and intellectual advantages of national independence, all the mutual benefits of a group of nations, stimulating, educating, correcting, and sustaining each other, with the internal peace and external security of a vast empire. And the same system which to all appearances is best for the Americans, is the best also for other nations brought into contact with them ; for without national divisions they will have no occasion to maintain standing armies; and without standing armies they, an industrial and frugal population, drawn with difficulty, as we see, from their farms and stores, will never be a source of danger to their neighbors. A federation, unlike a nation centralized in its capital, is capable of unlimited extension, provided that the federal principle be strictly observed, the central government confined to its necessary functions, and the local freedom of the several States scrupulously respected : a rule from which it is to be hoped that nothing which has now taken place will induce the Americans, against the dictates of their highest interests, to depart. The mere distance across the continent, where there are railroads, and no sea or alien territory intervening, can never prevent the meeting of a Federal Council for the necessary concerns of the Confederation. It is not to be forgotten that European Christendom was once, for important purposes, political and social as well as ecclesiastical, a confederation with the Pope at its head ; a state of things to which there is a growing disposition to return, though by a more rational and better road. On the other hand, if you could succeed in dividing the population of Central America into separate nations, and introducing among them, as your leaders propose, the "balance of power," that is, a system of international jealousy and suspicion, their state would be far worse than ours ; because divisions artificially created and sustained for purposes implying national hostility, would be far more bitter, and more productive of quarrels, than natural divisions caused by race and language, which of themselves imply no hostility, and which it is the object of all right-minded men to soften gradually away.   I believe that this fact has been present to the instinctive sense of the American people, in determining to face any present sacrifices, rather than consent to the permanent disruption of their nation.   And whatever may be the sequel of the war, the main object, in this respect, has been already attained.   The Slave-owners aimed at nothing less than the foundation of a vast slave empire stretching indefinitely westward and including Mexico, the mortal antagonism between which and the Free North would have ruined the tranquillity, security, and, to a great extent, the prosperity of the Continent forever.   All fear of such a result as this is now at an end.   Slavery will never cross the Mississippi.   If the Old States succeed in establishing their independence, which is the utmost that is now to be feared, they will scarcely be a power formidable enough to keep the Continent under arms.   Probably, as Slavery dies when confined to a limited area, they will sink, after a time, into decay.   The convulsive force which has been inspired into them, and the intense union into which they have been welded by the war, will pass away on the return of peace.   Facts, which those who have the destinies of the commonwealth in their hands, and whose duty it is to consider how far her powers can be pressed without endangering objects more valuable to the Americans themselves and to the world at large than the subjugation of the Old Slave States, will do well to keep before their minds.

The Americans are as well aware as you can be of the interest which the European Governments have, or imagine

they have, in producing disunion among the communities of
the American Continent : and they see plainly enough what
the consequences of giving an opening to European diplomacy would be. They find, directly their Union appears
likely to be dissolved, Canada goaded into an attitude of hostility on one side, and French ambition presenting itself in
arms upon the other. Your leaders exult in the prospect of
seeing a military despotism founded by the French Emperor
in Mexico, notwithstanding their righteous abhorrence of the
military despotism which they suppose to have been founded
by Mr. Lincoln in the United States. Perhaps the French
Emperor may have reason to wish that he had studied the
signs of political death before he assumed that the American
Commonwealth was dead. I am sanguine enough to believe
that one result of this dreadful struggle will be to bar for
the future all reactionary influences and enterprises of this
kind, and to make the new world a new world indeed, — a
world of new opportunities and new hopes for man. England — the English people at least — would be no loser by
the change : for no sinister influence, no artificial connection
which diplomacy can offer, is worth half so much to us as
our natural alliance with that portion of our race which has
the Western Continent for its dower.

Next, you appeal to our commercial classes, whose interests you say are involved in the recognition of the Slave
Power. I am glad that you do not leave our commercial interests out of sight, and I trust you will bear them in mind
when next the question of the Alabama and her consorts
comes under consideration ; for it is difficult to imagine anything more detrimental to the interests of a commercial
country, than the establishment of a principle under which
even an inland power might wage a maritime war against
us with impunity from neutral ports. There is in the Free
States an evil tendency to give protection to native manu-

factures, from which the Slave States are free, because they
have no manufactures to protect. We condemn this tendency
as decidedly as you can, and perhaps with more consistency
than noblemen and squires who a few years ago were resisting the repeal of the Corn Laws. But you have only to
glance over economical history to see that it is the besetting
sin, not of the Americans only, but of all new manufacturing
countries. It is as strong in Canada as in the United States.
The Americans are not wanting in shrewdness, and they
will learn in time, like their neighbors, that Protection is a
dead loss to the community, both in raising the price of com-
modities, and in diverting industry from the more profitable
to the less profitable employment. And then the only question for those who trade to America will be, in effect, as to
the comparative productiveness of free and slave labor, — a
question on which I abstain from entering, both because it is
too extensive, and because, so far as I am aware, all econo-
mists of eminence are on the same side. Meantime if you
think that the immediate interests of commerce would be
promoted by a great maritime war, with the sea swarming
with privateers chartered by our reckless hatred of the
North, Commerce, speaking by the mouth of her best representatives, appears to be of a different mind.

From commercial we pass to moral considerations. "The
struggle is one for independence on the part of the South,
and for empire on the part of the North." The struggle on
the part of the North, with deference to you, is not for empire, but for the maintenance of the existing Union, — a
totally different thing in every point of view ; as we, if we
had to put down a Repeal movement in Ireland, should very
clearly perceive. I doubt whether the author of the dictum
himself has failed to see the distinction since the battle of
Gettysburg. But suppose the North were really fighting
for empire. Are we the people to denounce and chastise

them for that offence?   Sermons in favor of continence are
very good things; but they are a little out of place when
preached by Lovelace, and by Lovelace fresh from a house
of ill-fame.   We grasp, in addition to our colonies, English
and conquered, and to our military dependencies, the whole
of India; we extend our rapacious arms to Burmah, and
try to extend them to Cabul; we annex, by robber's law,
Oude, Sattara, and Nagpore; we bombard Canton to force
a way for one set of our adventurers, and Kagosima to force
a way for another; we bayonet the last insurgent Sepoy in
cold blood; we deport the last Tasmanian to his island grave;
we baptize the Maories, exterminate them, and confiscate
their land, and then we turn round, and with uplifted hands
and eyes read Pharisaic lectures to our neighbors on the ex-
ceeding wickedness of fighting for empire.   And so with
"humanity," which you urge as a motive for getting us into
another war.   When has "humanity" prevented the English,
or any aristocratic or despotic government, from serving its
own objects, however selfish, at the expense of human misery and blood?   What say you to the crusade of our aristocracy against the French Revolution?   What say you to
the diplomatic war in the Crimea?   Has not the name
Peacemonger been as great a reproach here as it can be in
America?   Why are not these republicans to be allowed to
have their quarrels as well as kings and nobles?   This is
the first war for many a day in which the common soldier
has been fighting for his own cause, and in which, if victorious, he will share the fruits of victory.   Yet this is the
first occasion, so far as I am aware, on which the voice of
the English aristocracy and of the English clergy has been
raised in favor of peace.   The Bishop of my diocese called
upon his people the other day to pray for peace in America;
that is, for the success of the rebellion.   Full as the world
has been, since he has held the see, of dreadful and unjust

3   D

wars, he never bade us pray for peace before, and I doubt whether he will ever bid us pray for peace again. Our responsibilities are very extensive. But happily we are not answerable for the conduct of nations in America. We are not the censors of that continent, nor the arbiters of its destinies. Recent events ought to have convinced us that it is quite as much as we can do to remain arbiters of the destinies of Europe. Let us set an example of humanity in our proceedings, and we may be sure that the blood shed by great and independent Powers on the other side of the Atlantic will never be laid to our charge. Suppose that the North were likely to be guilty of holding the South as a "garrisoned dependency,"—a result which it is preposterous to predict in the case of Kentucky, Missouri, Tennessee, and the States beyond the Mississippi, all of which have been wrested by the Federals from that which you somewhat loosely and fallaciously call the South, in the course of the war,— let us take care that we are not guilty of holding Ireland as a garrisoned dependency. A good deal of the labor which we expend in setting the whole world to rights would be more profitably expended in doing some acts of justice within a narrower sphere.

Great Britain, you say, has been always ready to acknowledge a national uprising. That the British people have been ready to acknowledge and encourage national uprisings is true; but so far as I am aware, the sentiment has not before extended with anything like its present force to the aristocracy and the clergy. The love of patriot insurrection, if it has burned in the bosoms of those classes, has burned, till now, with a temperate flame. Italy, Hungary, Poland, Montenegro, have excited no such enthusiasm in aristocratic minds. The same may be said, I believe, of Greece; and I am sure of Belgium;—the two cases to which you specially appeal. The Christian nations crushed

under the brutal sway of the Turks are left to the mercies
of diplomacy without compunction. Venetia writhes beneath the yoke of a foreign oppressor; yet no aristocratic
association is formed for her deliverance. The Times cele-
brated with loud jubilation the triumphant entry of Ra-
detsky into Milan, and it loses no safe opportunity of showing
its hatred of Garibaldi, the great champion of nationality,
who now, through some unaccountable delusion, which has
led him to mistake his enemy's cause for his own, burns to
be fighting upon the Federal side. This is no uprising of a
nation. It is, and will always be called in after times, the
Revolt of the Slave-owners, who are trying to sweep away
the laboring part of what you call an uprisen nation into
irredeemable bondage, and who have forced their white
dependents into their armies by ruthless conscriptions, even
torturing British subjects, as our Government has expressly
declared, to compel them to enlist in their ranks. If it had
really been the uprising of a nation, it is doubtful whether
you would have got together all the present members of
your Association in support of the cause.

You offer, if we will assist you in establishing a great
Slave Power, to do your best to persuade the Slave-owners
to abolish slavery. I mistrust the offer, — at least I object
to going to war in reliance on it, — on two grounds, the
logical position of those who are to persuade, and the inflex-
ible resolution (as it seems to me) of those who are to be
persuaded. In this very manifesto you avow that man can
hold property in man; departing therein from the principles of your country, which denies the existence of such
property, and would set free at once, and in utter disre-
gard of the alleged rights of the master, any Southern slave
who touched her soil. Throughout this contest your party
have endeavored by all means and by every kind of argument, — Scriptural (of which the Times is a great master),

political, and physiological, — both in public and in private, to undermine the morality of the people on this subject, and to infuse into them the belief that Slavery, though open to some objections, was not a wrong. Worst of all, the attempt has been made, from which your Address is not entirely free, to destroy the moral confidence, and lower the moral bearing of England on the question, by persuading her that she was herself still tainted with the guilt; as though, if she " bequeathed slavery " to the Americans, she had not also bequeathed to them the example of abolition, and that at no trifling cost; and as though she were not yearly expending much money and not a few lives to put down the abominable traffic by which American slavery has been, and, if you can compass your object, will again be, fed. As to the Slave-owner, he is pouring out his blood and bringing ruin on his country for a cause which he has told us, in words which have made our ears to tingle, is the best on earth, — the cause of Slavery. And it has been justly said that, next to his fierce valor, the thing most worthy of respect about him is the haughty frankness with which he has avowed in the face of scandalized humanity his inhuman purpose, and spurned all the attempts of his more cautious advocates in this country to veil from the eyes of Englishmen the real object of the war. You talk in polite phrase of " servile labor," and " institutions distasteful to Englishmen "; but Slavery — perpetual and unlimited — is the name which he flings in your teeth as well as in ours. Like Danton, he has looked his crime in the face and done it; and his effrontery lends a kind of black majesty to his cause. Perhaps, indeed, he was sagacious as well as bold, and knew that a fierce denial of the Rights of Labor, though it would of course be met with professions of dislike, might touch a fibre of latent sympathy in reactionary hearts. Overtures, it is believed, have been already made by some

of your party to the Slave Government on the subject of
gradual emancipation : and it would be instructive, before
any serious step is taken, to know what reception those
overtures have met. But the truth is, that in your own
manifesto you furnish the Slave-owner with an overwhelm-
ing answer to any arguments, grounded on the moral evils
of Slavery, which you can possibly address to him. By
your own showing, Slavery, to your surprise and admiration,
has produced nothing but public and private virtue ; while
freedom has produced nothing but mendacity, cruelty, and
corruption. " Cast away, then," the Slave-owner will say,
"your English prejudices, however rooted they may be in
your minds by unsound legislation and irrational tradition,
and by your unwillingness to admit that your own emancipation of the slaves, so long your pride, was in fact an act
of stupendous folly. Accept the decisive verdict of experience, and, instead of truckling to an unsound public opinion
by imitating with a faint heart and stammering lips the language of the friends of freedom, unite with us in propagat-
ing an institution, the mother of every public and private
virtue, not only over America, but over the world."

Fail in your attempts to persuade the great Slave-owners
that it is better for their interests to give up their slaves, and
what will you have done by helping the Slave States to
establish their independence? Will you have created an
heroic republic, or an heroic community of any kind? The
military and administrative qualities which have been evoked
by the struggle, and which you admit yourselves that you
never perceived before the struggle, will cease to excite your
admiration or to excuse your sympathy with the Slave-owner
when the struggle is over. The decisive experience of history shows us that the consequence of Slavery to a nation is
death. You will have for a time perhaps continued displays
of military energy in filibustering enterprises, for which, as

Mexico and the West are cut off, the West Indies seem to offer a convenient scene. But afterwards, what can you hope to have but the loathsome spectacle of corruption and decay, — a vast Cuba, without the qualifying element of fresh blood from Spain? And the responsibility of this result will have been gratuitously brought by your efforts on a nation, which, if it was once deeply tainted with the guilt of Slavery, has perhaps done more than any other nation to redeem the slave.

Few people doubt that, if this war is allowed to run its course without interference, whatever may be its issue in other respects, Slavery will be abolished. The motives of the North for emancipating the slaves I once more decline to scrutinize. When there was a question as to our objects in insisting on the suppression of the slave-trade, Talleyrand said — and I have no doubt with truth — that he was the only man in France who believed that we were sincere. That a large and powerful party in the North at least was sincere, the Secession ordinances furnish, as was before said, irrefragable proof. Suppose the only motive of the North to be the military one of drawing off the laboring population which sustains the war: still, all men of sense who are hearty enemies of Slavery will be ready to welcome a great boon for humanity, through whatever accident it may be offered. We must not refuse to be saved from shipwreck because our preservers may have an eye to the salvage. Slavery was the bane and curse of that hemisphere; and its poisonous influence was beginning, as we see, to extend to some classes in ours. Let us accept its abolition at the hand of Providence, if we will not accept it at the hands of man. You think that emancipation would be better if effected by the free will of the master, deliberately and in peace, than as it is now being effected, by violent means, suddenly, and amidst the confusion of a great war. I think so too; but I know

that it is being effected in one way, and that it never would
be effected in the other.   And after all, unstatesmanlike as
it may appear, if the negro will work for wages, as there
seems so far reason to think that he will, there is no better
way of emancipating him than to set him free.   Incidentally
the war has proved very favorable in the highest sense to
the work of Emancipation, since it has led to the enlistment
of large numbers of negroes as soldiers in the Federal
armies, and has thereby perhaps done more than could have
been done within any calculable period, by any other agency,
to break through prejudice, and raise the social condition of
the long degraded race.*   The Emancipation Proclamation

* " The circumstances attending the departure of the Twenty-second
Infantry, a negro regiment, raised by the Union League Club here, for the
seat of war, three days ago, were a remarkable illustration of the strength
and rapidity of the tide of antislavery sentiment.   Last July it was for
nearly a whole week dangerous for a negro to show his face in the streets;
it is even at this moment dangerous for one to venture into some of the
Irish quarters; and when last autumn a colored regiment, raised in Mas-
sachusetts, was passing through New York on its way South, and it was
proposed that it should march down Broadway, the plan was abandoned
on the recommendation of Mr. Kennedy, the superintendent of police,
who said that if it were attempted he could not be answerable for the
peace of the city.   The war feeling and the antislavery feeling have been
rising so fiercely, however, ever since that time, that when the Twenty-
second was about to take its departure, it was arranged, not simply that
it should march down Broadway, but that there should be a public presentation of colors to it from the ladies in Union Square.   I walked down
to Fourteenth Street, to see the regiment march down from their quarters
at Pike's Island, on their way to the square in which the presentation
was to take place.   The square itself, and the parts of Fourteenth Street
bordering on it, the doorsteps, and lower balconies, and the sidewalks,
and all parts of the streets not kept clear by the police, were crowded
with colored people.   I never saw a tenth part of the number collected
together, and doubt if so many have ever been seen in one place at one
time in the North before.   The excitement amongst them seemed to be
intense; but I am bound to say that so orderly, well-dressed, and clean a
crowd I have never seen anywhere, though I have seen many crowds in
various countries.   The women, in particular, were very well and neatly
dressed, and had a most respectable look, in the best sense of the word.

was to produce a servile war with all its horrors, in spite of the affectionate relations which **at** other times we are told subsist between the masters and the slaves: but these ghastly visions **have** at least yielded to the sense **of** reality, and those who **cherish them are now** tired of shrieking in that key.

But **I am not sure that I have** not been wasting your **time and my own in going** through the paragraphs **of** your Address.   I suspect that the arguments set forth in it affect the minds of the majority of your party little more than they affect ours.   It is not a legal theory as to the rights of States under the American Constitution, — it is not a speculative view as to the differences of character and interest between the people of Richmond and the people of Washington, — it is not admiration of the Southerners, of whom, as I said before, so long as they remained in the Union,

The crowd was so dense that at some points it was only by great exertion that it was possible to make one's way through, and I was frequently hemmed in for some minutes, but I am satisfied I have never seen any collection of members of the ' superior race ' in New York close contact with which would not have been ten times more offensive than with this congregation of ' niggers.'   A New York Irish crowd of the same size, in the same place, would have been unapproachable by anybody with the use of his nose left him, and retaining an ordinary regard for the safety of his skull and ribs.   When the regiment marched round the corner from Fourteenth Street, the band playing and colors flying, the enthusiasm of their friends passed all bounds.   One mulatto woman standing near me looked on eagerly for a few minutes, and then burst into tears, and all along the line, as far as I could see, white handkerchiefs were being shaken frantically by thousands of sable arms.   They marched very steadily, in heavy order, and were generally of very fine physique, — finer, I think, than the .average of white regiments, and there was much greater equality amongst them in age.   Many of them were of huge proportion.   I noticed two or three sergeants tall enough and brawny enough for Barnum's Museum.   Their weak point was the handling of their muskets, which were badly carried and clumsily shifted; but I learned that they had only been furnished to them ten days previously, so that they had had little time for drill.   The officers are all white, and have been selected for this regiment with great care.   Many of the captains seemed nothing was too abominable to be believed, — it is not a desire to bestow on Central America the blessings of separate nationalities and the balance of power, — it is not a romantic affection for Free Trade and a passionate abhorrence of Protection, — it is not a newly-born though laudable sense of the wickedness of fighting for empire, — it is not an enthusiasm, if not newly-born, new in its intensity, for the cause of insurgent nations, — it is not a fear lest Slavery should be extinguished in any manner but the most statesmanlike and the most conducive to the highest interests of the negro: — it is not any one of these things, nor the whole of them put together, that has kindled among the reactionary party in this country a passionate and almost frantic excitement of feeling, such as has not been witnessed among the same party since the war against the

---

very young; but the field officers are, I believe, all West-Pointers, and have seen service. In front of the Union League Club a platform had been erected, and from this an address to the regiment was delivered by Charles King, the president of Columbia College, and a stand of colors was presented on behalf of a body of ladies belonging to ' the best society.' Bouquets were flung to the officers; the colonel led in three cheers for the club and the ladies, and they then marched down Broadway amidst a general huzzaing and waving of handkerchiefs along the whole route. The marching of the men during this part of the progress was very fine, — steady, vigorous, and correct. They wore the United States blue and white leggings. You see the world moves, after all. I saw two respectable-looking colored men shake hands as the regiment moved off from Union Square, one asking: ' Well, what do you think of this?' ' I like it; I like it,' was the reply; ' and I thank God I 've lived to see it.' As regards the value of these troops for military purposes, I may mention that General Seymour, who commanded at the late battle in Florida, is an officer of the regular army, and has been a very virulent proslavery man, full of contempt for negroes, says, in a letter to a friend in New York, speaking of the affair of Olustie: ' The colored troops fought splendidly, magnificently. One fellow, a color-sergeant in his regiment, stood holding the colors of his regiment until he stood almost alone, and then he fell covered with wounds.' " — *New York Correspondent of the Daily News, March 23, 1864.*

3 *

French Revolution; that has caused the special organs of
these classes in the press actually to foam with fury, and to
forget the interests as well as the duties of journalism in
their attempts to keep on a level with the passions of their
readers; that has made the legislators of a great maritime
and commercial country hail with loud cheers the success of a
precedent rendering every neutral port a basis of operations
for our enemy in time of war; that has incited members of
the British House of Peers to stand forth publicly and avow
themselves leaders of a league having for its object the
"disruption" of a friendly nation, allied by recent treaties,
and bound by common objects of public morality to our
own; that has thrown the Conservative party in this country into the arms of the Democratic mob of New York;
and that has led men careful of their character to face the
finger of suspicion, which will always be pointed at the aristocratic allies of the Slave-owning aristocracy of the South.
History will not mistake the meaning of the loud cry of
triumph which burst from the hearts of all who openly or
secretly hated liberty and progress, at the fall, as they fondly
supposed, of the Great Republic. How senseless that cry
was; how absurdly mistaken they who raised it were in
thinking that the rupture between Slavery and Free Labor was the effect of republican institutions, and betokened
their ruin, matters little: the source of the joy which rang out
in it was not doubtful. It has sunk now to a lower and less
jubilant tone. The Commonwealth, the first hour of weakness being past, has put forth a power and displayed resources which have astonished not only her enemies, but her
friends; and it seems as though, after one bright glimpse of
hope for Slavery, the evil spirit of Freedom were about to
prevail in the world once more. That issue, fraught, as it
is imagined, with fearful consequences, can now, apparently,
be averted only by dragging England into the war upon

the Southern side. And this may yet be accomplished: It will be accomplished, without a shadow of doubt, if the rams escape from the Mersey, and proceed to prey from an English port on American trade. The more vehement members of your party **see** their opportunity, and are trying to take advantage of it ; while your great organ in the press labors earnestly to keep up the mutual exasperation which, if a dispute should take place, would render a peaceful solution almost hopeless. But before you, the great friends of " humanity," from whom we have had such impressive homilies on the horrors of war, plunge us into a war with America, think twice whether it is wise for you, looking to your own interest, to do so. For, depend upon it, if you make a mistake, it will be one of the most serious kind.

The minds of some, no doubt, are still full of the recollection of the crusade against the French Republic : and they think **perhaps** that the same game might be played with success again. But in those days, Parliament being unreformed, the Tory aristocracy, and their ecclesiastical confederates, had absolute command of the nation. It signified nothing what blunders were committed, or what disasters were encountered, — what armies were lost under the Duke of York in Flanders, or what fleets were driven to mutiny at the Nore by reckless corruption and **mismanagement**, — what financial burdens were imposed upon the country. The mass of the public were almost as passive instruments in the **hands** of the dominant class, though under the form of a free constitution, as the **American** slaves are in the hands of their masters. Moreover, the lower classes were so sunk in ignorance, that it was easy to work upon their passions, and to persuade them that the French, their ancient enemies, were coming to cut off their ears and noses, and to force them to eat frogs instead of bread. The taxation was grinding ; but the misery to which the people were reduced only made them the more willing to enlist: and those by whom, and for whose objects the taxes were imposed, got the greater part of their own payments back in the shape of the high rents and high tithes produced by the protection which the war gave to home-grown corn, and were further indemnified by sharing among them a vast patronage both in Church and State. The wealthy merchants who supported the Government also prospered, through the monopoly of commerce secured to them by a war in which we were completely masters of the sea, — a monopoly most injurious to the helpless many, but very profitable to the influential few. Any fiscal burdens which would really have entailed sacrifices on the holders of political power were thrown off upon posterity. Toryism was absolutely in the ascendant, and all incovenient aspirations, all thoughts of political or social reform, were for the time effectually extinguished by the fury of the war.

I do not say that you would not be able to do the same thing again: but I say that it is doubtful whether you would be able, and that the question deserves your deliberate consideration. We have not yet got a Free Parliament, but we have a Parliament very far less enslaved than the Parliament of Pitt, and one which, in case of miscarriage and suffering, may become, as it did even in the Crimean war, the organ of discontent. There is far more intelligence and political activity than there then was among the working classes in the towns, and these men are, for the most part, as well aware that the cause of those who are fighting for the rights of labor are theirs, as any nobleman in your Association can be that the other cause is his. Our peasantry are of course still very ignorant on political questions: but they have no natural antipathy to the Americans; they would not be so easily persuaded that the Americans were coming to cut off their noses and make them eat frogs: perhaps it has begun

to dawn upon them that, if there is any danger of being
forced to eat frogs, it arises from a different quarter: and
emigration is now turning the thoughts of the more adventu-
rous of them away from the army, in which I believe they
are with some difficulty brought to enlist, — a serious consideration, since the noblemen of your Committee will not go
to war, except in a metaphorical sense, and you must still
fight your battles with plebeian blood. As to Ireland, you
would have to hold it, in the plain language of the Duke of
Wellington, as a conquered country: and I need not say that
the Americans possess far greater power of working on disaffection there than were possessed by the French, more
especially as the priests were opposed to the alliance with
the French, whom they regarded as the enemies of their
religion. Nor perhaps are the men of rank who head your
Committee likely to allow enough for the actual connection
between a great number of families of the laboring class
on the opposite sides of the Atlantic. "Burn down New
York!" said a laboring man the other day; "New York is
the home of my two brothers and my married sister!"
There was no difficulty of this kind in the French war. The
safety-valve of emigration, which carries off a very explosive
force from Ireland, will be closed, and the explosive force
will accumulate at home. You have most of the great merchants on your side, so far as sympathy is concerned: but
they begin to feel that they would be called upon to undergo
sacrifices such as only very strong sympathy will endure in a
war in which we could not expect to be absolute masters of
the sea: and our commerce, since its great extension, and its
wide ramification under the system of free trade, has become
far more sensitive than it was in the time of Pitt. The
national debt would scarcely bear addition, and you would
have to lay upon the country a burden of taxation which
nothing could render tolerable but victory. It is unpatriotic

to magnify the powers of an antagonist : but it is prudent to measure them, and I can scarcely imagine any one doubting that the powers of our antagonist on this occasion would be such as to insure us a long war, more especially as the seat of action would probably be fixed, very much to our disadvantage, on the Canadian frontier, at a great distance from our base, and inaccessible to reinforcements during a great part of the year. These are not the days of Bull's Run, when Pennsylvanian regiments were marching away from the sound of the cannon. Adversity, as I said before, has done its work ; and the feeble braggart, as he once appeared, stands before you a strong and truly formidable man. The force and genius of the American nation has by this time been fairly thrown into war; its best men, selected by a process terribly searching, are at the head of its armies ; and those armies are composed of soldiers whose blood and sinews are British, who form in the British line, and go into action with the British cheer. Probably there are almost as many men of British birth under arms in America as there are in England. But that which appears to me, who am incapable of forming a judgment on military questions, most formidable in the American Commonwealth, supposing that its destruction is your object in the war, is that, as I said at the outset, I suspect that this Great Community of labor bears in it, with all its faults, something not uncared for in the councils of Providence, and which Providence will not let die.

Therefore, before you let out the rams, consider the chances of the game, and think whether the stake is really worth the hazard of the throw. It is true, no doubt, that if the American Commonwealth survives and prospers, its example may in the end affect the political and social system of this country. But the operation of this influence is probably as yet very remote ; and you may feel pretty confident that the con-

vulsive effort of this war, and the vast expenditure entailed
by it, will be followed by a period of collapse and financial
perplexity, sufficient to guarantee you against contagion for
some years to come.   Meantime, I am not sure that America
does not contribute, as a safety-valve, to your security more
than she adds to your peril as an example of prosperous
freedom.   Even in the time of Charles I. it is not improba-
ble that the crisis would have arrived earlier, but for the out-
let afforded to Puritan discontent by the New England colony, and the prospect which that colony held out to those
who remained behind of a deliverance from Charles and
Laud, independent of revolution : so that you may be repeat-
ing, under another form, the folly which the reactionary
Government of those days committed when they stopped
the vessel full of Puritan emigrants in the Thames.   Your
real danger, if danger it be, lies nearer home.   The aristocracy of this country, as an exclusive and hereditary branch
of the national Legislature, is almost, if not quite, left alone
in Europe.   The feudal tenure of property, with primogeni-
ture and entail, is very fast disappearing in every European
country but ours.   Long before American institutions will have
had time seriously to infect us, our nobility will be called upon,
upon more direct and pressing grounds, to show that the continuance of a system essential to the existence of their order
on its present footing is also compatible with the economical,
social, and moral interests of the people.   Nor can I imagine
that the success of Free Religion (supposing it to be suc-
cessful) on the other side of the Atlantic can be a source of
rational apprehension to the Established Church comparable
in magnitude to the theological convulsions which are already
tearing her vitals here.   All these questions, and that of the
enfranchisement of the people, may yet be settled, as every
right-minded man, however desirous of reform, would wish
them to be settled, by calm discussion, tranquilly and amica-

bly, in the common interest of all classes and orders in the nation. But if you persist in your present course, and attain the end towards which you are now driving, they will perhaps be settled by political struggles which, like those produced by the reviving desire of Reform after the peace of 1815, will bring us to the verge of civil war.

Remember, in conclusion, that it is only an honest neutrality which we ask. We ask no aid, direct or indirect, for the Federals. We do not deprecate the strict enforcement against them of all the laws of war, in case they should do anything contrary to our obligations as neutrals. We condemned the outrage on the Trent, and supported the demand for redress as cordially as you did : though we did not think that the communication from the American Government, assuring us of an amicable solution, ought to have been suppressed. We do not even deprecate war, disastrous and fratricidal as it would be, if the Federals refuse to respect our rights or our honor. What we ask is, that you will not abet the Southerns as you are now abetting them, in the attempt to drag us, by means of these piratical vessels, or by any other means, into an unjust and dishonorable war. If you do, and if, in the war which ensues, you fail speedily and decisively to crush the American Commonwealth, you may give, though in an evil way and before the hour, a great impulse to political and social progress here.

I am, &c.,

GOLDWIN SMITH.

Cambridge : Stereotyped and Printed by Welch, Bigelow, & Co.

www.ingramcontent.com/pod-product-compliance
Lightning Source LLC
Chambersburg PA
CBHW022023080426
42733CB00007B/696